HOMELESS

This book is to be returned on or before
the last date stamped below.

LIFE FILES

HOMELESS

HAMILTON
COLLEGE

JUDY BASTYRA

Evans

EVANS BROTHERS LIMITED

Published by Evans Brothers Limited
2A Portman Mansions
Chiltern Street
London W1M 1LE

© copyright Evans Brothers Limited 1996

British Library Cataloguing in Publication Data.
A catalogue record for this book is available
from the British Library.

First published 1996

Printed in Hong Kong by Dah Hua
Printing Co. Ltd.

ISBN 0 237 51633 0 (paperback)

Author's note:
I would like to thank the following people in
particular for their help during the research and
writing of this book: Tessa Swithinbank of The Big
Issue, Katrina Phillips of CHAR, Gillian Golan of the
Leaving Home Project, Centrepoint, Isobel Olsberg
and David Ferguson. I would also like to say a
special thank you to Charles Bradley, Ruth Thomson
and Karen Testa for their tremendous support.

The Author and Publishers would also like to thank
Michelle Dixon of Crisis, Dr Dragana Avramov of
FEANTSA (Fédération Européenne d'Associations
Nationales Travaillant avec les Sans Abri - European
Federation of National Organizations working with
the Homeless), Nicholas Fenton of Childhope, Rev.
Derek White of St. Cyrian's Church, 'Youth
Homelessness' by Jacqui McCluskey, published by
CHAR (Housing Campaign for Single People),
Charing Cross Police Station, The Children's Society,
The Coalition on Homelessness, Emmaus, The Grand
Central Partnership (New York), Health Action for
Homeless People, Homeless International, London
Connection, Marie Stopes International, Missing
Persons Bureau, National Coalition for the Homeless,
Oxfam, Plan International UK, The Refugee Council,
Save The Children, The Sheffield Gypsy and Traveller
Support Group, Shelter, Young Homelessness Group.

ACKNOWLEDGEMENTS

Editorial: Rachel Cooke and Su Swallow
Design: Neil Sayer
Production: Jenny Mulvanny

Cover James King-Holmes
page 7 John Birdsall **page 8** David Hoffman
page 10 Maggie Murray/Format **page 12**
Martin Adler/Panos Pictures **page 15** Barbara
Laws, John Birdsall **page 17** Michael Ann
Mullen, Format **page 18** Ulrike Preuss/Format
page 20 David Hoffman **page 22** Philip
Wolmuth/Panos Pictures **page 25** Andrew
Ward, Life File **page 26** The Times, Rex
Features **page 27** David Hoffman **page 28**
Crisis **page 29** Maggie Murray, Format **page
30** Sue de Jong, Format **page 32** John Birdsall
page 33 The Hutchison Library **page 34** Philip
Wolmuth/Panos Pictures **page 39**
Range/Bettman/UPI **page 41** David Hoffman
page 42 Press Association/Topham **page 43**
John Birdsall **page 45** David Hoffman **page 47**
Paul Smith/Panos Pictures **page 48** David
Hoffman **page 49** Jacky Chapman, Format
page 51 Paula Solloway, Format **page 53**
David Hoffman **page 54** Jean Fraser **page 57**
Ulrike Preuss/Format

CONTENTS

WHAT DO WE MEAN BY 'HOMELESS'?

WHAT IS A HOME?

Homeless means without a home. A home is a place of shelter. It protects us from the weather and other dangers lurking outside. In this sense, home has not changed since our earliest history. But for most people home has come to mean more than just a shelter.

A home is a secure, permanent place with an address you can give to other people. It is a place where you can keep possessions safely. It is often a place shared with family, who provide a different form of security. A home also has the facilities for everyday life – cooking and eating, sleeping, washing and going to the toilet. As technology has developed, the standard of these facilities has improved and with them our expectations of what is necessary in a home. How many of us today think of a television or a washing machine as a luxury?

Perhaps most importantly, a home is where you can relax and have

Question

'Home is where the heart is.'
'An Englishman's home is his castle.'
How true do you think these sayings are? Does 'home' mean the same thing in each saying?

Eating together as a family at home is an activity that we often take for granted. It is one of the things that homeless people miss the most.

some privacy. It is somewhere you can choose how you want to live – although you may have to do this alongside your family. In your own home, you can be tidy or messy, and decorate as you please. If you don't want to see anyone, you can close the door. A home is a place which is your space. If you have a home you probably take these things for granted. To be homeless is to be without all these things.

and hostility. They have no family to turn to in a crisis. In the UK and other developed countries, it is very difficult to get a job without an address (see page 33) and, without the money from a job to pay the rent, it can be very difficult to get a home. Today, more and more people are discovering what it means to be homeless.

WITHOUT A HOME

The world is a very different place for homeless people: there is no safe place to keep their things, no bed for the night, there's nowhere to wash, eat, cook or go to the toilet. They are constantly in danger from assault, verbal abuse, illness, cold, hunger

WHO ARE THE HOMELESS?

The image that most of us in the developed world associate with homelessness is that of the vagrant or tramp.

Vagrants or tramps are an accepted part of our 'developed' society. They are mostly middle-aged men, more often than not they have a drink problem or a mental health problem. They can be quite frightening, with

It is not only men who live on the streets. This bag lady in San Francisco is representative of the growing number of women who now live on the streets.

> **The problem is how to turn the tramp from a bored, half-alive vagrant into a self-respecting human being.**
>
> *Down and Out in Paris and London*
> George Orwell, 1933.

long hair, ragged clothes, be dirty, smelly, drunk and sometimes abusive. Indeed, it can be difficult to feel compassion or sympathy, despite the good reasons why such people appear as they do (see Chapter 2).

It is perhaps the changing profile of homeless people in recent years that has led to homelessness becoming one of the most critical social problems in the developed world. More and more young people, single mothers and families are finding themselves homeless. The sight of an old man passed out on a park bench surrounded by empty beer cans may be something that society is used to but nowadays you are just as likely to see a young person with nowhere to go except some doorway.

LIVING IN A DOORWAY

If you take home to mean simply shelter, then many of the homeless do find or create for themselves a home. For three years David's 'home' was a doorway, his bed a concrete slab, in The Strand in the West End of London. His story highlights many of the issues that surround the homeless today:

'I ran away from Scotland when I was 16. My father had lost his job through drink –

he also lost his pension, his mortgage, my mam and the house. My mam, sister and I were rehoused in one room in a bed and breakfast. We fought all the time. She found the situation of losing her home and me being a difficult teenager too hard. So, one day after a particularly bad argument, I just packed my bags and left – hitching my way to the bright lights of London. I had no qualifications, very little money, just a backpack and a sleeping bag. I asked the driver where to go. He told me to go to The Strand, where there were other homeless people.

I couldn't get a job, so I began begging. I couldn't claim any benefits as I was only 16. I couldn't afford to rent a place because I didn't have a job. Some days, especially when the sun shone, I was happy but when the weather was bad it was horrible. Soon people would turn away from me as I passed by – I smelt so bad. One day I got caught in a rain storm; I got really soaked. I dried out but you know what it's like, your clothes get really musty. I went into a shop to buy something but I was thrown out of the shop because I was told that I was making the staff sick.

I was arrested 21 times for begging, then I was put into prison. It was sheer living hell – but that's when I got in touch with my parents again because I had an address for the first time in three years. My mam and dad were back together. They asked me to come back home but the streets had changed me. I was no longer their wee boy anymore. I was a man now, but I keep in touch with them. It's hard being on the streets but it's even harder getting off them.'

Question
Do you think David was right to leave home when he did? Would you do the same thing?

> ❝ **Since the break-up of the Soviet Union in 1991, about 50,000 have become homeless in St Petersburg alone.** ❞

David's is a universal story. In city centres all over the world, you see bundles of rags in doorways that are homeless people wrapped up in sleeping bags or blankets, trying to keep warm. You also see them begging in underground passes, shopping malls and railway stations. Cardboard cities are commonplace – colonies of homeless people living under bridges in temporary shelters made from cardboard boxes, pieces of wood and blankets.

THE HIDDEN HOMELESS

You don't have to be living in a cardboard box to be homeless. Society is well aware of the homeless living on the city streets, because they are so visible, but not all the homeless

> ❝ **In 1994 in the UK, 4,740 households were living in bed and breakfast hotels. The housing charity Shelter estimates that this represents over 13,600 individuals. The cost of providing this accommodation for local authorities is estimated at £65 million per annum.** ❞

are so conspicuous. Many homeless people find themselves sleeping on friends' floors, some families have to live back with their parents in cramped, unsuitable accommodation, whilst others live in hostels or bed and breakfast hotels. Some end up squatting, that is, occupying an empty house or property illegally (see page 31). These people are often referred to as the 'hidden homeless'.

Homeless people are not just found in cities. There are many people in rural areas without a home and the so-called 'New Age' traveller, who may have some kind of van as a home, faces many of the same problems as the city homeless (see page 30).

STREET PEOPLE AROUND THE WORLD

Although homelessness is an international problem, an issue to be faced by different cultures throughout the world, views of it are not always the same. In many developing countries, where the numbers of homeless have been much higher for longer than in richer countries, homelessness is questioned less. The homeless are seen as having no alternatives. There are many who are born on the streets to street people, and to these people, homelessness or having a makeshift home is the only way of life they may ever know.

The numbers of street people are growing – in 1950 in Bombay, in India, there were 20,000 pavement dwellers, today the figure is estimated to be 1.5 million. Savita's home is a makeshift bamboo hut built on a narrow pavement strip in Bombay. Her story is not unlike those of street dwellers found in other

To some people, the streets are the only home they have ever known. Many of the pavement dwellers in Bombay were born on the street and have no hope of ever having a home of their own.

Asian countries, as well as those of Africa and Central and South America.

'I've lived on the streets of Bombay for over 20 years. I ran away from home when I was just 15. My family were wealthy, we had a big house with servants to look after me. But my parents were both violent people – they often beat me. Whatever I did was wrong. One day I just decided to go. I stole my mother's savings and took a few belongings and left for the big city – Bombay.

I soon made friends with a family who allowed me to sleep outside their tent and in return, I fetched their water for them. I met Sunil, now my husband, on the streets. I asked Sunil to marry me because I was afraid to be alone on the streets. He worked as a construction worker when he could find work and I worked as a domestic. He'd run away from home when he was 11. He wasn't even sure if his large hungry family even noticed.

Our first home on the streets was a wooden booth that was a barber's shop by day and our shelter at night. We then moved to an archway after our first child was born because we needed shelter during the day as well as night. We have been here now in Sofia Zuber Road since 1972. When we first arrived there were only a few families but with each new arrival, our space became smaller. There are now 50 families.'

Question
What are the differences and the similarities between David's and Savita's stories?

Question
Do you think it is more acceptable that there are people living on the streets in Bombay than in London?

'WE LEFT BECAUSE WE HAD TO'

Poverty, war, famine, epidemics and political instability throughout the world have created a very different type of homelessness, that of thousands of people suddenly fleeing their homes and sometimes their countries, to save their lives. Many become refugees.

A refugee is defined by the United Nations as a person who 'owing to a well-founded fear of being persecuted for reasons of race, religion, nationality, membership of a particular social group or political opinion is unable, or, owing to that fear, is unwilling to avail himself of the protection of his own country.' These people seek asylum in the

> 66 We were playing at about 5 o'clock when these people, the soldiers, came. We just ran. We didn't know where we were going to, we just ran. 99
>
> A 14-year-old Sudanese refugee describes how he left his home village.

more stable environments of other countries. Others who have fled their homes but have not crossed an international border are known as 'displaced ' people. Generally their situation is in every other way identical to that of refugees.

Tired after days of walking, these people had to flee their homes and abandon their possessions due to civil war, only to look forward to a life in a squalid refugee camp.

Many groups have been refugees for years, sometimes decades:

- **2.5 million Palestinians** ejected from their homes more than 46 years ago
- **One million Tamils** half of them in southern India, half in the West, uprooted from Sri Lanka since conflict erupted there in 1983
- **More than one million Liberians** escaping civil war since 1989
- **More than three million people** in Croatia and Bosnia are refugees or are displaced
- **One million Somali** in Kenya, Ethiopia, the Gulf and the West have been forced to flee because of hunger and lawlessness
- **More than one million Sudanese** are refugees or displaced by their country's 30-year civil war

We tend to think of refugees as living in camps far away, but there are many refugees living here in our own country. Thousands of former Yugoslavians, together with Somalis, Sudanese, Romanians and Vietnamese are trying to make a new life here. Apart from losing their homes and friends, many have enormous problems because of cultural and language barriers when they first arrive. Some are unqualified, which may also make it difficult to find employment, which in turn affects their ability to acquire suitable housing. Others are highly educated but do not have the right qualifications to work in their profession in their new country. These include young people on their own as well as entire families.

A LEGAL DEFINITION

One of the most confusing aspects of homelessness is the fact that in different

> **" There are more refugees in the world than at any other time in history. The figure stands at a record 23 million. More than half of them are children. Another 25 million are displaced within their own country. "**

countries homelessness is defined in different ways. This makes it difficult to have accurate comparisons of levels of homelessness between countries and sometimes to assess the extent of the problem.

British law is unusual in Europe because it gives an exact definition of the homeless (see panel on page 14), and this definition is then separated into further categories of homeless people. Only families and single parents have statutory rights. Single homeless people are not entitled to the same help. But in some countries, such as Greece and Italy, the existence of homeless individuals or families is not recognised. Unless they can be categorised under a different social problem, such as being a runaway, suffering from violence, or being a political refugee, homeless people cannot apply for help from the state.

In the United States, definitions of homelessness vary from state to state, as

> **" In the 15 Member States of the European Union at least 2.5 million (more likely 5 million) are homeless. "**

does the help they are entitled to. Many of the 'hidden homeless' are often not defined as homeless. As we shall see later in this book, this question of definition plays an important role in the status of homeless people in a particular country and the help they are entitled to.

Definition of a homeless person in Britain

❝ **If they have no accommodation they are legally entitled to occupy; they have accommodation but cannot secure entry to it; they are liable to threats of, or actual violence from someone living there; or if it is not reasonable for them to continue to live in their present home.** ❞

The Housing Act 1985, Part II

Question
How would you define 'homeless'? If you were homeless, what do you think you would miss most?

WHOSE PROBLEM IS IT?

Few people would argue that it is a problem to be homeless but, as the number of homeless people increase, there is a growing argument about how this problem should be tackled and by whom.

Many people blame the government or the social services, for neglecting these people in need. Some think it is the result of the recession and the loss of jobs. But many others feel that, particularly in developed countries, the homeless have a choice – that it is their own fault and they could find a home if they wished. They should 'get a job like other people. Why should society be responsible for them?'

In this book we look at the many different causes and consequences of homelessness and the issues arising from them. We attempt to explore why it is happening in our modern society world-wide. We hope to encourage people to discuss the problem and the different ways of approaching it and to decide for themselves who should take responsibility for solving it.

WHY DO PEOPLE BECOME HOMELESS?

To start to find solutions to homelessness, its causes need to be identified. This is by no means easy – homelessness does not just happen to a particular 'sort' of person. The reasons why people become homeless are as varied as the people themselves.

However, beyond the many individual factors, there are some underlying social trends which research into the causes of homelessness has identified. Some are the result of a particular government's housing policies, others are simply factors that have become an increasing part of modern life, such as marriage break-up and changing patterns of employment. It is clear, too, that throughout the world poverty plays a major part in creating a homeless population.

> 66 By and large such (homeless) persons are drawn from those sectors of the population which could be labelled 'disadvantaged'... We cannot emphasise enough that those who become homeless are often people who already experience high risks of social marginalisation. 99
>
> Third report of the European Observatory on Homelessness, 1994

HOUSING POLICY

Most governments today have some kind of approach or policy concerned with providing housing for its people. This could be anything from helping to finance the building of new homes, to encouraging people to buy homes that they have previously rented from the state. Housing policies are complex and they differ considerably from country to country.

Many people are without a home, yet houses and flats stand empty and boarded up.

One criticism that is levelled at all the countries in the developed world where homelessness is a problem is 'lack of affordable housing'. Why should this have happened in countries which have a large proportion of the world's wealth and when houses are often sitting empty? In France, for example, there are nearly two million empty flats and houses – yet more than half a million homeless. There are a series of factors that have contributed to the decrease of available homes for those on lower incomes:

• Privately-owned rented accommodation is far less readily available than it used to be and tends to be much more expensive.

In 1960 in the UK, for example, 30 per cent of all homes were rented from privately-owned property. By 1988, this figure had dropped to 10 per cent.

• There is a growing trend away from the state investing its money in public or social housing. This means that the number of new homes built and owned by the state has decreased in several countries. These are the homes which are normally available to people who cannot afford to rent or buy privately.

• Some governments, notably the British, have privatised parts of the rented social (council) housing sector, selling off property which could be set aside for social or public housing either to individuals or to housing associations. This means that there is less state-owned accommodation available, even though demand for it is high as a result of increased rents in the private sector.

• Benefits available for those on low incomes to pay for housing (see page 33) have become increasingly restricted, whilst rents both in the private and public sectors have gone up. It is easier now for landlords to evict (that is, throw out) tenants who cannot afford to pay the rent. However, it is easier still for a landlord to select tenants offering the best financial guarantees, for example, someone in full-time employment may be favoured above someone who is unemployed.

CHANGING LIFESTYLES

It would be simplistic to say that all the factors listed above are purely a result of government policy, or that governments alone can be blamed for the increase in homelessness. Most developed countries are controlled by democratic governments chosen in elections by the people they govern. As such, their policies should reflect the wishes of a majority of the people. They should also reflect and respond to changes in the way society works as a whole.

Since the Second World War, life in the home has changed considerably. Families are smaller but fewer people live under the same roof. In the past it was not unusual to have three or four generations of the same family living together. Today it is much more likely for grandparents, parents and children over 18 to live separately. Many more young people now choose to live on their own or with friends. About two in five marriages in the UK now ends in divorce, too, and both parts of

the broken family will need a home. All of this means that there is far more demand for accommodation and housing than in the past, which in turn enables landlords to charge higher rents for what is available.

Throughout the developed world, people now need to look and travel further in search of work, with no guarantee of success. Unemployment has become a longterm problem for many countries, with technological advances leading to industries employing fewer people to do the same job and periods of recession causing redundancies and business closures. Patterns of employment have changed and people can no longer rely on the concept of a job for life with one company – always assuming they manage to find work in the first place.

In rural areas, changes in farming methods have resulted in fewer jobs for people and a rising homeless problem. Farm cottages for farm workers were a major source of housing in the past. Now there are

> **66** A (homeless) man in his 30s described how he had been made redundant from his first job after three years. 'It was a shame that it fell to pieces really. I'd be a foreman by now.' After an unsatisfactory second job he moved to London in the 1980s, 'looking for pavements of gold... I didn't find them.' **99**
>
> *We are human too, a study of people who beg*
> Alison Murdoch for Crisis

Waiting for the job centre to open. Finding a job is not easy for many people, but for the homeless, who have no address, nowhere to wash and make themselves presentable for interviews, it is practically impossible.

fewer jobs, many farmers find it more profitable to sell off their cottages for holiday homes and commuter/retirement homes rather than rent them to local people. The demand for this kind of housing has also forced the property prices up in rural areas and made it more difficult for local people to afford to buy.

All these underlying factors have contributed to the shortage of housing or the lack of money to pay for it and this in turn has led to homelessness. But there are also more personal causes of homelessness.

EVERYONE IS DIFFERENT

No two homeless people's stories are the same, but they may have certain things in common. People often become homeless through a

> **Three months ago my wife and I had a home which went with our job, which was running a pub. Unfortunately, what with the recession, business was slow. We lost the lease and the business loan. We've not only lost our jobs but our home as well. We're in a catch 22 situation: without a home you can't get a job and vice versa.**
>
> Tom, who used to run a pub with his wife Mary and lived above it.

Just because you are homeless does not mean to say that you are no longer interested in the world about you.

series of events – personal crises or tragedies – that have knock-on effects. An extreme example might be: a man loses his job which leaves him unable to pay the rent and he and his family are evicted. The man becomes depressed and he begins to drink heavily. This puts pressure on relationships, and his marriage breaks up. Caught up in a downward spiral of hopelessness, the man eventually ends up on the streets. But, more often than not, far fewer ingredients than this can lead to homelessness. Sometimes, it can simply be that a home is part of the job and that goes when the job goes.

A MATTER OF CHOICE?

Many people in society feel that the homeless have a choice, that if they got a job, stopped drinking or taking drugs, they could find a home. In fact very few people choose to be homeless. The few people who do choose to live on the streets are mainly those to whom 'homelessness' has become a way of life. Generally it is the older people who have found the companionship of other homeless people preferable to being shut up in a room or flat by themselves – the middle-aged single man or woman, the 'tramp' or 'bag-lady'. Many of them have been institutionalised for most of their life – as children, in care or in foster homes, as adults, in prisons, or in military institutions (the army, navy or airforce). Those with mental health problems will have spent time in hospital. In such institutions, many of the responsibilities of every day life – from doing the shopping to paying the rent – are taken care of by someone else. There are always other people around to give companionship and support, almost like a family. On leaving these institutions, some people find it hard to adjust to the outside world and end up on the streets.

A recent report by Crisis revealed that four out of ten older homeless men and women had been in the forces or institutions of some sort. One in three suffered mental illness. Another common reason for their homelessness was loss of a partner through divorce or death. In Britain, it is currently estimated that 19,000 people with mental health problems are homeless, in temporary accommodation or in prison. It is as great a problem among young people as in adults. The illnesses range from mild depression – making people tired, negative and unmotivated – to severe psychosis. This may involve people hearing voices,

> " I'd been in the army for twenty years. I trained as a cook. I never had to pay any bills. Had my board and keep looked after. All the food was free. Good mates all around me. I travelled the world. When I left the forces my life fell apart. My marriage broke up. I started drinking and couldn't keep a job. Couldn't cope alone. Felt so lonely. Ended up on the streets. I've always got someone to talk to. Four of us share a big doorway. When you sleep on the pavement you can't sink no further. All you have to do is get up in the morning. "
>
> Peter, a middle-aged homeless person

Find out!
What is a catch 22 situation? Why can it be applied to homelessness?

seeing things which are not there and violent behaviour. The majority of mentally ill people found on the streets are people who have been in short-term psychiatric hospitals, for a few months only, rather than the long-term patients. But these short-term patients need considerable support from family or local authorities when they leave hospital. If this is not forthcoming or a person fails to take advantage of it, homelessness can be one possible outcome. But when Crisis interviewed people who beg, only two homeless people out of 145 said they did not want a place to live.

Many of the homeless who sleep rough are suffering from mental health problems. Even if support is available, they may not take advantage of it.

LEAVING HOME

It is estimated that there are 156,000 young people who are homeless each year in Britain. And the number is growing. Within the European Community as a whole, there are approximately one million homeless under the age of 21.

As with older people, there are some young people who choose to be 'homeless', to squat, become travellers or sleep rough rather than live in hostels or other accommodation that they have been offered. But in most cases the young homeless do not have these offers to turn down. Perhaps more than any other group, the growth of

> ❝ The young homeless are a low priority for both agencies (housing and social services departments) and when myths are combined with widely held negative attitudes and stereotypes, the young homeless are often denied the necessary services, are 'blamed' for their homelessness or seen as 'trying it on'. ❞
>
> *The Guardian*, 5 August 1994, in an article based on a report on homelessness funded by the Nuffield Foundation called *Breaking the Spiral*

in benefits for young people leaving home to be cut back (see page 34) and an often unsympathetic response from local government agencies (social services and housing departments) when young homeless apply for help.

But research shows that most young homeless people have left home for a range of reasons, some negative, known as 'push' factors, and some positive, known as 'pull' factors.

youth homelessness is a result of the social trends and changing government policies.

Leaving home should be part of the natural process of growing up. Young people leave home when they are ready to be independent. But living independently is not cheap. Apart from the rent, there are bills, food, fares, and clothes, to be paid for. Many young people are unaware of what is involved in looking after themselves and can find themselves in deep financial trouble if they have had no previous experience of budgeting. They can lose their home because they simply do not have enough money to live on. They may not realise that when renting accommodation you have to pay at least one month's rent in advance and also a deposit. If they cannot raise enough money, they may be forced to squat or, as a last resort, to sleep rough.

Some people believe that young people leave home for the fun of it, to have easy access to better housing and generous social security benefits. In the UK, this has resulted

THE PUSH AND PULL FACTORS

The pull factors are relatively simple to identify. A young person may leave home to look for a job, to study or to be near friends and some, particularly those in rural areas, are drawn to the excitement and options of big cities. Many feel that their opportunities will be greater in the metropolis.

The push factors are the elements in a young person's own home that make it desirable or indeed necessary for him or her to leave. It is often the younger teenagers – runaways or throwaways (see panel on page 22) – who leave home for the 'push' factors. Their youth, often coupled with disadvantaged backgrounds, means they are the least prepared for the realities of independent living.

> ❝ Most young people who become homeless are either thrown out or forced to leave for their own safety. ❞
>
> *The Guardian*, 5 August 1994 (see above)

> A 'runaway' is a young person who is away without consent. A young person aged under 16 cannot live legally on an independent basis in the UK. A 'throwaway' is someone who has been thrown out by her or his parents or carers. Runaways or throways are not necessarily homeless.

During adolescence children often find themselves in conflict with their parents or carers. The struggle to find independence can lead to arguments. They might want to stay out late at night, or their parents/carers may disapprove of their friends and the way they behave. Each day there is a new issue to argue about. Sometimes the battle becomes so great that leaving, or running away, seems their only choice. Once they have left home, even if they want to go back, many of them feel they will lose face if they do so, or they simply do not know how to make the first step to contact their family again.

When young people run away from home they often do not realise how expensive it is to live in a big city. They soon run out of money and do not know where to go for help. Many of them resort to begging in the underground just to feed themselves.

> **I was abused by my grandfather since I was 12. I told my mum about it two years ago. Her first reaction was something like 'he is the last person to do such a thing.' It became impossible for me – I had no-one to turn to, if my own mum didn't believe me. The only way I could escape from the situation was to leave home – run away.**
>
> Sue, a young homeless woman

parent enters the family during the young person's early teens. Another large and growing problem among teenagers is their sexual identity. Young lesbians and gay men can feel forced to leave home, either because they are unable to tell their family about their sexuality, or because they are rejected by their family.

YOUNG PEOPLE IN CARE

Another common push factor is negative experiences of being taken into care and of the care system itself. Many of the youngsters who are homeless have been in care: that is, for various reasons, they have been taken away from their families and placed under the care of the state, either in children's homes or with foster parents. Some children have been moved constantly from one centre to another and have found the situation difficult to cope with. Many just want to be independent and do not want to be subjected to rules and regulations, much in the same way as other adolescents who live with their families. But, as with older homeless people, children who have lived in institutions for much of their life and who have no family network to fall back on find living independently extremely difficult.

For others, leaving may have more serious causes. It is frequently a response to an unbearable situation, such as physical or emotional abuse. Their departure can be sudden and unplanned. Many of these young people are unable to return once they have left and without the safety net of a family to return to, they face a high risk of becoming homeless. In a recent report, it was shown that 40 per cent of young women who are homeless have been sexually abused, in many cases by a relative or family friend.

This situation is one of the most difficult for a young person to deal with. For many of them the person abusing them is someone they trust. In some cases a parent may even know or suspect that it is happening but also does not know how to deal with it. So running away seems like the best solution.

Thousands of homeless people come from backgrounds where the families have split up through divorce. Many young people experience difficulties with relationships with step-parents, especially when the step-

> **Centrepoint Emergency Hostel in London says that two out of five of the homeless young people they see have been in care. Fifty per cent of these are aged 16 or 17.**

> **❝** I was in care since I was a young girl. My mother couldn't cope with us. She was ill. But I had a mum, many of the other kids didn't. She also spoke with a posh accent. The carers couldn't understand why I was in care, I was middle class. None of the other kids had a mum like mine. I never got on with the carers or the other kids, they bullied me. Somehow I was different. When I left care – I just couldn't cope. I still can't. My mother doesn't want to see me. I don't know how to look after myself – to cook, clean, budget, pay bills. I've been institutionalised all my life. I've lived in hostels for the past 12 years – I couldn't live by myself. I just couldn't function in society! **❞**

A young homeless person

Find out!

Try to work out how much money you would need for a week living on your own. Find out typical local rents, and add the cost of food, travel and other essentials. Allow enough for water, heat and light, too.

STREET CHILDREN

The problems of the young homeless are far more acute in the developing world. Rio de Janeiro, Manila, Calcutta, Mexico City and Nairobi now all have a massive population of children who grow up on the streets. Their lifestyle bears little or no resemblance to what most children in the developed world experience as their childhood. From a very young age they have to exercise their survival skills and many do not live to adulthood. They live alone or in packs on the streets, the beaches or in makeshift homes on rubbish dumps. It is not unusual to see a 5 or 6-year-old sniffing glue or smoking. Even the cities without a history of street children such as those in eastern Europe and the former Soviet Union are now experiencing the dilemma of street children. St Petersburg, for example, is estimated to have 10,000 homeless children sleeping rough.

As in the developed world, some of these children have left home to escape sexual or physical abuse and have little or no contact with their families. Others have been made orphans through war, epidemics and illnesses such as AIDS. But the major cause of the large numbers of homeless children in the developing world is poverty: many children have been abandoned by their parents, who were just too poor to look after them, and the state is unable or unwilling to provide support for them instead.

WHERE DO THE HOMELESS GO?

THE BRIGHT LIGHTS

Cities are magnets to the homeless. In chilly Vancouver, Canada, the homeless find comfort around the heating vents of shopping malls. In Paris, the metro offers a respite from the cold. There are homeless people to be found in cardboard boxes close by the glass-and-concrete high-rises of Tokyo's financial centre, and near abandoned factories in Sydney and Melbourne. It seems that throughout the world, cities draw poor and homeless people to whom the bright

The bright lights of big cities like New York attract homeless people. But life on the streets is far from easy, whether in town or country.

lights represent hope, work, fun – a future. Often when they get to the big city they find out that it is not what they thought it was. Cities rarely resolve problems for the homeless, but many still prefer to stay.

Many homeless people go to city centres for the simple reason that they know that there are other homeless people there. Because of this, they know that there may be some sort of infrastructure for helping the homeless: food, clothes, blankets and medical care. These services are available through day centres, health centres, agencies and charities (see page 60). If they want to find a place to sleep there are numerous options in hostels, night shelters and refuges. There is also a regular transport system, whereas in the countryside transport is

infrequent. There may be only one or two buses a day to reach any welfare centres and it may be too far to walk. In the city, if people cannot find work and run out of money – there are always crowds to beg from.

WEATHER WATCHING

The weather is a big factor determining where the homeless go. In the summer, parks, fields and public gardens provide a haven.

It does not take long to find out where other homeless people live. It seems that almost every city has its own 'cardboard city', a community of homeless people.

However, all around the world, many people object to seeing homeless people living in public areas. This has resulted in legislation banning inviduals from sleeping in many of these public areas. In some instances, the homeless have been hosed down with water to wake them up and move them on. In some countries a more violent form of persuasion is used.

In warm weather many of the homeless in the cities sleep in temporary shelters that they have built themselves. They often call these shelters 'bashes'. Bashes are made from boxes and pieces of wood, cartons, blankets and bits of plastic. One or several people may be living in them. For added protection, bashes are often found under bridges and, in places like this, large communities of

> " In the day I go to the London Connection (a day centre) to relax and do stuff like swimming. The staff are my friends and are trying to help me get my own place. "
>
> Sarah, aged 16

homeless people can develop, creating the so-called cardboard cities.

As the weather becomes colder the homeless find other places where they can keep warm. Many rough sleepers will try to

St. Botolph's Crypt for the Homeless provides facilities for the homeless during the day. Many churches offer respite from the cold and provide a place to socialise.

Question

If you ran a hostel for the homeless, what rules and regulations, if any, would you create?

find a place in a hostel. This is a type of temporary accommodation which provides people with a bed for the night. Some are provided by housing and religious charities, others are state-funded and a few run simply to make a profit. In Britain the cost of the accommodation is usually met by housing benefit, paid direct to the hostel. Hostel users may be asked to pay for extras such as breakfast from their income support.

Hostels vary enormously. Some allow you to stay for one night only, while others provide a temporary home for days, months, even years. Many of them have strict rules and regulations: no drinking or drug-taking, no riotous behaviour and usually a time that you have to be back at night. These rules are needed to help provide a safe environment for many different types of people. Some hostels cater for certain types of users, for example, young women, families, ex-offenders or people with an alcohol – or drug – dependency. Here, trained staff seek to assist these people with their problems.

Most hostels only provide a homeless person with a place to sleep and are closed during the day. In the cities, particularly during bad weather, some homeless people go to public libraries – if they are allowed to – but others go to day centres. These are often connected with churches, which can provide space in their buildings for the centres. At the centres, a homeless person can receive medical care, and help with finding work and accommodation. Sometimes a meal is also provided. Importantly, too, people can benefit from the companionship and support of others in similar situations to themselves.

Voluntary soup kitchens are an essential part of the support system for the homeless, especially during the cold weather.

BED AND BREAKFAST ACCOMMODATION

In the UK, another form of temporary accommodation can be provided by bed and breakfast hotels. Many homeless families are offered this type of accommodation by local authorities while waiting to be rehoused. Bed and breakfast hotels usually provide one room, access to bathroom facilities, and breakfast. Some rooms have cooking facilities but generally kitchens are shared between several people. Children usually have nowhere to play, apart from the bedroom. Families may have to wait up to two years to move on to more suitable accommodaation.

In the United States, some states will provide the money for homeless people to stay at hotels or YMCAs (Young Men's Christian Association hostels), but the accommodation is only available for periods of 28 days at a time.

A single mother and her child living in one room in bed and breakfast accommodation, waiting to be rehoused.

> **❝ I was sleeping on a friend's bedroom floor for a year waiting for a house. I was pregnant at the time. In the end I got a truck and got out. ❞**
>
> Sarah, a traveller

> **❝ New Age travellers? Not in this age, not in any age! ❞**
>
> John Major, Prime Minister of Great Britain, Conservative Party Conference, 1992

ON THE ROAD – A POSITIVE MOVE?

In a report issued by the Children's Society it was revealed that 'a number of young homeless people were moving – either individually or in small groups – from sleeping rough into vehicles and caravans, thus becoming travellers. The young people concerned perceived this as a positive move.' But is travelling really preferable to homelessness?

Being a traveller is not a new way of life. Records show that Romany Gypsies have been in Britain since at least the 16th century and other traveller groups have followed their arrival. However, the latest group of travelling people, New Age

Some people prefer the lifestyle of New Age travellers to a more conventional lifestyle. Others become travellers as an alternative to being on the streets and alone.

travellers, is one of the hardest to define. They differ from Romany Gypsies, Irish and French travellers and the Spanish 'transeuntes' in a number of ways: they have a much shorter history; they are not defined as a distinct ethnic group under the Race Relations Act; they do not necessarily follow traditional routes of travel; and adult travellers have rarely been born into travelling, though there are increasing numbers of children of New Age travellers growing up as travellers.

In society, New Age travellers are generally defined as being hippies and peace campaigners. They are associated with convoys, festivals, new and eastern philosophies and religions, and, increasingly, with green politics. They seem to attract a lot of adverse publicity: they are seen as irresponsible people, who steal and create rubbish, and their mobile homes and convoys are portrayed as offensive blots on the landscape.

However, the report from the Children's Society goes on to say that, without exception, travellers in the study who had previously been in bed and breakfast accommodation or unsatisfactory housing considered the travelling lifestyle to be far preferable. This was particularly true of traveller women with children, who gain considerable support and help from living in the travelling community in caring for their children. This sense of community is one of the main attractions of the travelling lifestyle. For some it is seen as an alternative lifestyle, a way out of the consumerism and materialism of modern society, giving freedom to the individual.

Question

'New Age travellers are parasites on society.' What do you think?

SQUATTING

Throughout the developed world, at any one time, there are always thousands of houses and other property standing empty. Indeed, the number of empty properties usually exceeds the number of homeless! Some of this property is empty simply because landlords cannot find people prepared to pay the rents they want. In other cases, property may be awaiting development and its owners (be they private or the state) do not have the money or sometimes the will to do this.

However, some people take advantage of this empty property: rather than sleeping on the streets, going to hostels, or travelling, they squat. A squatter is someone who lives in an empty property without the consent of the owner.

In the past, some squats were established for such a long time that the residents were able to buy the properties very cheaply and

> 66 A lot of my friends squat. We don't squat because we want to, but because we have to. Renting a flat is completely out of the question. There is a deposit to pay plus one month's rent in advance. The only money I have apart from my grant and student loan is about £20 a week from working in a bar over the weekend. 99
>
> Mick, a student and squatter

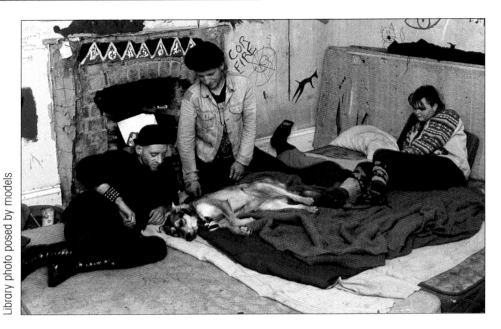

Library photo posed by models

Squatting may sound fun to some people – having your own house for free – but in reality squats can be cold, dirty, even rat-infested, and lack all basic amenities.

they created housing cooperatives to share the cost of mortgage payments. These housing cooperatives are now one source of good, cheap accommodation but, as a result, there are long waiting lists to join them. However, in recent years, many countries have tightened up the laws on squatting (see page 50), making it easier for owners to remove squatters from their property, so these long-term developments are less likely to happen.

Squatting in the developed world can seem quite attractive to young people, who may feel as if they belong to a kind of club. The buildings that are empty and used for squatting may even be in reasonable condition. But in many other countries, squatters use buildings that are no more than shells – derelict, bombed-out skeletons such as those in the war-torn cities of Beirut or Sarajevo. When people are struggling for survival they will live anywhere.

In some developing countries, whole towns have been built up from people squatting not in empty property but on empty land. This happens particularly outside large cities where large numbers of poor people have moved in the hope of finding work, which often does not exist. Soweto, the township outside Johannesburg in South Africa, started life as a squatter city, and there is a huge squatter city outside Rio de Janeiro in Brazil.

Question
Do you think homeless people should have the right to squat? How would you deal with squatters if you owned an empty property?

Find out!
Contact a hostel or day centre for the homeless. Find out what sort of people use it, what rules and regulations there are and what help and facilities are provided.

HOW DO THE HOMELESS SURVIVE?

As we have already established, one of the chief causes of homelessness is poverty. But once on the street, the homeless still need money for food and other essentials.

The obvious solution to this problem would be to find a job, but this is far from easy. It is practically impossible to find work if you are homeless, because you do not have an address for correspondence when applying for jobs. If you are sleeping rough, it is even more difficult, as your appearance can be off-putting, leading to a rejection even before your actual qualifications for the job have been considered. However, some homeless people try to earn money by shining shoes, washing cars and washing windscreens at traffic lights. Some find casual work handing out leaflets or selling magazines (see page 57).

In the developed world, homeless people who cannot find work often obtain financial assistance through the state-financed benefit system. Benefits vary hugely from country to country, and, in the USA, from state to state.

Life in the streets is degrading. Even basic necessities are hard to come by and many end up going through rubbish bins for food and items to keep themselves warm.

WHAT ARE THE BENEFITS?

The general benefits that are available to homeless people from the Government in the UK are Income Support (if they are not working), and Housing Benefit should they find accommodation. They can also apply for other benefits depending on their age, health or situation. For example, you can get free medical and dental treatment if you are on Income Support. This is benefit for people who do not have enough to live on. It is paid by the Department of Social Security (DSS). In 1995 the basic rate for a single person aged 18-24 was £36.80 a week. Over 25

A family in the single room they have shared for a year in a hostel for homeless families.

Other benefits available to certain homeless people include Unemployment Benefit, One Parent Benefit, Disability Living Allowance and a Community Care Grant.

Some homeless people do not claim benefits because they are either too proud or too embarrassed. Others are simply unaware that the benefits are available. Given their circumstances, it is often also likely that homeless people do not have the right documents with them. In order for anyone to claim benefits they have to have some form of identification – for example, in Britain, a birth certificate, National Insurance card or passport.

years of age, the basic rate was £44.50. The amount people can claim depends on their circumstances: their age, whether they are single, have any children, or have a disability. Only in exceptional circumstances can people under the age of 18 claim Income Support.

Housing Benefit helps to pay a person's rent. But it does not cover the cost of meals, heating, hot water or lighting. A person on Income Support qualifies for full Housing Benefit. Most full-time students are not entitled to claim Housing Benefit, although they were able to claim in the past – the change has meant that students have to rely far more heavily on grants, government loans and parental support than before to finance their accommodation.

TOO YOUNG TO CLAIM?

In Britain, many of these benefits, however, are not available to 16 or 17 year-olds who leave home. This is partly to encourage this age group to remain at home longer and, if they have left school, to participate in the training schemes on offer.

But many young people do leave home, and it is not always easy for them to find work or places on training schemes.

In autumn 1994, unemployment among under-20s was 19.2 per cent, for 20 to 24-year-olds it was 14.6 per cent. The national average for all ages was 8.9 per cent.

These age groups can apply for the short-term benefit of Income Support – once on it they must reapply every 8 weeks. Claimants qualify if they face 'severe hardship' without it. But there is no legal definition of 'severe hardship', so local social services can interpret this in different ways.

The benefit may not always be easy to claim, but many teenagers are not even aware of the benefit in the first place.

In 1995, the Coalition on Young People's Social Security, a coordinating body of more than 30 charities, reported that 85 per cent of staff in the group had worked with teenagers who did not know about the severe hardship payments.

CAN BEGGARS BE CHOOSERS?

Some homeless people obtain money by begging. Until fairly recently, begging was a rare occurrence in the developed world. Nowadays, however, it is hard to travel in any city without someone asking you for

> **There is no justification for it [begging] these days. I think it is an offensive thing to beg. It is unnecessary. So I think people should be very rigorous with it.**
> John Major, Prime Minister of Great Britain, 1994

money. Many people find it unacceptable and react angrily.

John Major's remarks (see panel above) came two weeks after a newspaper report of a 'homeless' beggar earning up to £80 a day. Some of the ex-homeless people interviewed for this book said that there are people who do exploit the situation, but stories about earning hundreds of pounds by begging on city streets were absurdly exaggerated and could only serve to encourage youngsters to beg rather than look for work.

The charity Crisis produced report in 1994 entitled 'We are human too: a study of people who beg'. According to this report, begging is generally used as a means to 'top up' income that comes from benefits and the average takings in a day are between £10-£20. It is seldom enough to live on.

> **It's called severe hardship because it's severely hard to get hold of.**
> A young claimant for Income Support, Times Educational Supplement, 24 February 1995

> **It's nonsense that beggars can earn huge amounts of money. Maybe that can happen occasionally, at Christmas perhaps, but whenever I've booked beggars, none of them had more than £3 on them.**
> An urban policeman who works in a homeless unit

Laws against vagrancy and begging still apply in, for example, Belgium, France, and the United Kingdom. In this country the Vagrancy Act of 1824 was originally passed to stop veteran soldiers of the Napoleonic Wars begging, the punishments for which included flogging and imprisonment. Today, beggars are usually fined, although persistent offenders may be sent to prison.

WHAT IS WRONG WITH BEGGING?

It is not simply because begging is illegal that it provokes such controversy. Many people react badly to it because of the unpleasant feeling it gives them – many feel uncomfortable to see begging in what is regarded as an affluent or developed country. A person begging is a physical reminder that there are other human beings like ourselves who are in need of help, yet we are not always prepared or able to give it. We often find it difficult to know how to react, feeling angry, embarrassed, confused or guilty. Begging, too, carries a social stigma: like prostitution, it is something we feel people should not do.

Many of us also feel that the homeless would rather beg than work, but the Crisis report shows that two in five people who beg have applied for jobs in the past year and the most common single wish of people begging is for housing, followed by work.

Another reason for not responding to people who beg is the widely-held belief that any money given will be spent on drink and drugs. It is true that many people who sleep rough do have drink or drug problems and one third of people begging have a recognisable substance-abuse problem, usually alcohol. However, one of the most common reasons for using alcohol or drugs is to counter depression and loneliness (see page 41). This is true for people who are not homeless, as well. The only difference between these people and the homeless is that they have the privacy of a home in which to drink or take drugs, away from the eyes of other people.

In reality, according to the Crisis report, the most common item bought with begging money is food (see table below).

> " It is not the beggars but the begged-from – you and I – who twist upon the rack. "
>
> Bernard Levin, *The Times*

Items bought with begging money	% of people who spent money on any item
Food	69
Bills	5
Rent deposit	1
Travel	30
Alcohol	47
Entertainment	8
Gambling	9
Tobacco	64
Rent	9
Toiletries	24
Clothes	33
Drugs	26
Fines	8
Other	9

Question
If a person on the street asked you for money, what would you do? What other things could you do to help them instead of giving them money?

With no way of finding work to get money this man has turned to begging.

In the Crisis survey, only six people out of 145 claimed to have enjoyed begging at some stage. Seventy-six per cent found it extremely difficult and humiliating to start with and 50 per cent of these continued to hate it, while the remainder became resigned.

As these statistics reveal, few people enjoy begging so most choose to do it from financial necessity. The longer they beg, the easier it becomes but also the harder it is to stop and the longterm damage to a person's self-esteem can be considerable. This is true not only for people who beg but anyone

Find out!
In Victorian Britain, homeless and unemployed people were sent to the local work house. Find out about what a work house was and how it operated.

living on the streets on a longterm basis.

How else do the homeless survive? Some are buskers, although busking is illegal without a street entertainers' licence. Some homeless are desperate enough to break into cars to steal radios, bags, or whatever they can find, and some turn to prostitution.

LIVING OFF RUBBISH

In the developing world there are few, if any, benefits available for homeless people. Begging is one of the most common ways by which they support themselves but many of the poor and homeless people eke out a living by recycling rubbish, plastic bottles or rags. Children in many places are expected to help their families by working. It is not uncommon to see a child as young as five or six working, either by themselves or helping their parents, often collecting rubbish from dumps for recycling.

In India, children who collect rubbish for resale are known as ragpickers and it is estimated that in Delhi, they clear as much as a quarter of the city's rubbish for recycling.

But the Delhi Corporation has recently banned the trade on the grounds that the ragpickers are a health risk and disrupt the running of the city official rubbish collection (which is far from efficient). The ragpickers are the city's poorest children and come from the lowest caste of Indians known as the Untouchables. Many people despise the Untouchables and it has been suggested the ban is more to do this than with any disruption they cause.

> **66** My family and I have lived off the dump for 10 years now. We came to the city from our village looking for work. We ended up here as the last resort. We built a hut using material we found on the dump and I sell the plastic I collect from here each day. At least we eat here – in the country we couldn't pay rent for the land and eat. **99**
>
> Eliza, a child living on a rubbish dump in Guatemala

With his sack of finds from Guatamala city's main rubbish dump a young boy passes a group of vultures and wades through discarded packaging from a fast-food store.

> **66** Ragpickers make India one of the world's least wasteful societies. **99**
>
> *The Times*, 5 May 1995

WHAT DANGERS TO THE HOMELESS FACE?

Survival on the streets is not just a question of money; homeless people also have to contend with more immediate dangers to their well-being. Firstly, they face a constant battle with their health. And, secondly, without the security of a home or family, they are far more likely to be the victims of abuse, physical attack and the other criminal activities associated with a big city's streets.

IS IT HEALTHY TO BE HOMELESS?

The simple answer to this question is no. As a result of their lifestyle, the homeless are more likely to suffer from certain physical and mental illnesses than the rest of the

A homeless man lies under a plastic sheet in Washington, USA, across the street from the White House, during the first snow of the season.

population, and it can be difficult for them to get access to health services. Sleeping outdoors and lack of sanitation both contribute to ill-health, as do poor diets and irregular eating habits. There is a high incidence of digestive complaints among the homeless, including stomach problems, ulcers, constipation, diarrhoea and vomiting.

When you have flu, you feel awful: your head hurts, your bones and back ache, but if you rest and keep warm you will usually recover after a few days in bed. But for a homeless person it is not so easy – sleeping out in bad weather, unable to keep warm or clean, and eating badly as well, can turn a dose of flu into a serious and debilitating illness. Weakened in this way, a homeless person is also more susceptible to other illnesses and infections, leading to a continuous circle of ill-health.

Chest and breathing problems are typical among the homeless, in particular bronchitis, lung cancer and tuberculosis (TB). One study found that homeless men are 50 times more likely to suffer from TB than the rest of the population. Doctors worldwide warn that a lethal drug-resistant strain of tuberculosis could spread among the homeless. Crisis recently screened 250 homeless people in Britain and results suggest that as many as one in 50 are contaminated.

> ❝ Personal hygiene is such a problem that nits, fleas and scabies are commonplace. But right now the biggest problem we have to deal with is Hepatitis B. ❞
>
> Social worker at a London day centre

Question
If you were homeless, what would you eat? How would you wash? Where would you go to the lavatory?

This level is even higher than in New York. In 1993 there were 6,052 reported cases of TB in the UK and around 400 related deaths. Homeless families in bed and breakfast accommodation, especially children, may suffer from asthma, development and other problems from living in crowded, often damp and poorly ventilated conditions.

Rough sleepers experience a higher level of muscle and joint problems, and foot and back pains. Imagine sleeping on a cold, hard, damp surface night after night, having one pair of shoes and having to walk everywhere. The author Robert Swindells lived on the streets for a while, researching his awarding-winning novel, 'Stone Cold'. His book captures the physical discomfort of sleeping rough:

> ❝ I found a doorway. A good deep one, so deep that light from street lamps and shop fronts didn't reach the door itself and you could sit with your back against it and not be seen by passers-by... But by eleven my feet and legs were cold, I was tired, my bedroll was giving me a numb bum and I was dying for a pee ... ❞
>
> Extract from *Stone Cold* by Robert Swindell, reproduced with the kind permission of the author and Hamish Hamilton Children's Books (1993)

STRESS ON THE STREETS

As we have seen, mental health problems can be a cause of homelessness, but they are as likely to be a result of it.

Stress is linked to many health problems and all homelessness creates high levels of stress. For instance, not knowing where your next meal is coming from, where you are going to sleep, and not having anyone to rely on are all very stressful.

Stress in turn can lead to depression and, without proper care and support, this can be very hard to combat. Poor physical health and exhaustion can also lead to depression. The suicide rate amongst the homeless is very high.

The homeless are 34 times more likely to commit suicide than someone who has a home. Suicide accounts for nearly a quarter of all deaths amongst the homeless.

A CURE FOR DEPRESSION

Many problems with mental health and physical health are interlinked and it is often difficult to separate cause and effect. Drugs and alcohol abuse amongst the homeless contribute to the vicious circle of ill-health. Some people become homeless because they have a drink or drugs problem, but many homeless people use drugs and alcohol to lessen the pain and misery of their situation.

Abuse (that is, excessive use) of drugs and alcohol can cause and contribute to both

▶ page 43

> **The worst thing is the loneliness. Just having no one to trust and love. What I would like most is a dog. I've got to love dogs since I've been in this situation. There are barriers with people but not dogs. They are trusting and not judgemental. I just wish there were more hostels that would take pets.**
>
> Laura, 25, a homeless person

Loneliness, and the stress of trying to survive on the streets, can lead to depression.

> **Imagine what it is like, if all you have to look forward to at the end of the day is sleeping in a doorway or in a hostel with drunks, nits, scabies, fleas, noise, smells, wouldn't you want to obliterate it with drink or drugs?**
>
> Helper at a youth day centre

> **The average life expectancy of a person living rough is 47. The normal average life expectancy is 73 for a man and 78 for a woman.**
>
> Crisis report, *Sick to death of homelessness*

A homeless man makes the best of what shelter he can find. It is perhaps not suprising that so many homeless people turn to alcohol for comfort from the cold.

THE RULES OF THE STREET

> **I had to have a few cans to give me courage before I started begging. When I was into drugs real bad, smack, speed, I would do anything to get the money. That's how I started turning tricks …**
>
> Young male prostitute

Sleeping rough is always dangerous. There is no door to shut to keep you safe. You have to learn to look after yourself. Some homeless people have been attacked and even killed by other street dwellers – for money, identification documents, drugs, sleeping bags or even cans of beer. And the homeless are easy targets for abusive or violent gangs.

In the midst of these uncertainties and dangers, it is perhaps not surprising that certain rules for life on the street emerge. As with the rules at school, these are an attempt, if rather more informal, to impose order on a particular society. If you break the rules at school, you are punished; the same is true of the rules of the street, but the justice administered can be rougher.

The main focus of the rules is a respect for territory. If a homeless person has a particular area or place (pitch) where they beg, it is not done for someone else to be

mental and physical health problems, for example liver and heart disease. There are also added risks in drug-taking, such as overdosing and sharing needles (which transmits diseases such as HIV), risks that are perhaps higher in a street situation. There is, of course, a high chance that a heavy user can become addicted. Addiction can lead to dangers not only associated with health.

SITTING TARGETS

Homeless people are extremely vulnerable, physically and emotionally. This is particularly true of the younger homeless. They arrive in the city unaccompanied and knowing no one and so present an easy prey to men wishing to exploit them for money or abuse them sexually.

Whilst it is possible to over-dramatise this problem, it is a very real one. Most western cities now have special police units who are on the look-out for young people who may be vulnerable, particularly runaways.

> **These kids are happy to find someone kind. They have no idea what lies ahead of them – more often than not they get drawn into prostitution and other vice rings.**
>
> A policeman working at Charing Cross Station, London

Amusement arcades act as magnets to many homeless young people, but they also attract people who prey on the young.

> **Life on the streets is very dangerous. Many young people think there is a sort of glamour attached to it. You know, being in a gang, belonging to the underworld. Let me tell you – I see kids coming here to the day centre on a daily basis. It's Sodom and Gommorrha out there. And don't let anyone tell you otherwise.**
>
> Social worker in day centre for young people

there, too. A sleeping pitch and bedding are equally seen as the property of one particular person and to be respected as such by other street dwellers. Similarly, in cities where street gangs operate, each gang has a well-defined territory which other gangs do not trespass on. In some cities, these gangs can also operate as taxers, terrorising beggars in their areas and demanding at least 30 per cent of their takings.

The realities of living on the street are harsh. The homeless can and do derive great support from each other but, in the struggle for survival, it is hardly surprising that violence sometimes occurs.

Question
If you were homeless, how would you keep healthy and safe?

DO THE HOMELESS HAVE ANY RIGHTS?

Rules, respect, territory – all these words are concerned with how society as a whole operates. Another important word is right, that is, something to which you are entitled, legally or morally. Legal rights are those which are embodied in the laws of a particular country. Many of these laws have been created to uphold what are seen as moral rights. These are much harder to define, as morality – that is, what is seen as the correct way to live – varies with culture and beliefs. The street 'taxers' for example (see page 44) may see the money they take from people begging as their right – most other people would not agree. However, some rights are generally recognised as applying to all people, regardless of their differences. These are called human rights. They are embodied in the Universal Declaration of Human Rights, drawn up by 48 nations when they met in 1948.

In theory, the homeless have the same human and moral rights as everyone else, but in practice this does not always happen. The laws of a particular country may make it difficult to force other people to uphold these rights, or may favour one person's right above another – as we shall see, it is never easy to see where one

> 66 **All people are born free and equal, and should behave with respect to each other.** 99
>
> Article 1 of The Universal Declaration of Human Rights

Living on the streets, sharing each other's company, can create a bond of mutual support and friendship.

person's right begins and another's ends – and no amount of legislation can ever eliminate individual prejudices. Like many other minority groups, the homeless are often treated badly by people who consider themselves to be superior to the homeless. Some people see the homeless as people who have chosen to become outcasts from society and as such not entitled to the same rights as those who have remained part of society.

An extreme example of this attitude was seen a short time ago in Bogota, Colombia. Notices were put up in one of its most deprived neighbourhoods of Bogota, inviting people to attend the funerals of street children (see below).

These planned murders of children of the street were commonly referred to as 'social clean-up operations'. They were carried out by armed vigilantes who took it upon themselves to eliminate so called 'undesirables': the drug addicts, thieves, guerrilla suspects, prostitutes, homosexuals, the mentally ill and the gamines. In 1994, Amnesty International reported that up to 40 children were being killed every month – they were usually shot and their bodies buried in unmarked mass graves.

Similar human rights abuses against street children have been reported in Brazil and other developing countries. International pressure created by groups such as Amnesty have helped to curb the violence at present by publicising it, but the problem has by no means disappeared. And these attitudes are not exclusive to developing countries (see chapter 5).

A RIGHT TO HAVE A SAY?

The respect that is due to fellow human beings is by no means the only right that the homeless can lose. In many countries, they lose the right to vote by not having an address.

The loss of the right to vote is called disenfranchisement and in many countries this can happen simply by failing to register to vote. In order to register in the UK, as with all other European Union countries, you need to have an address – an obvious problem for a homeless person. In Manchester, the City Council are helping the homeless to be eligible to vote by allowing

> 66 The industrials, businessmen, civic groups, and community at large in the Zone of Martyrs invite you to the funerals of the delinquents of this sector, events that will commence immediately and will continue until they are exterminated. 99

> 66 Everyone has a right to take part in the government of his or her country, whether by voting or being an elected member of parliament. Fair elections should be held regularly, and everyone's vote is equal. 99
>
> Article 21, the Universal Declaration of Human Rights

These people in Nicaragua have travelled miles to register their vote. In many countries a person without an address cannot vote.

them to register a 'locality of residence' rather than a specific address. In the USA, policies differ from region to region, but out of its 50 states, only four actually have written laws giving homeless people the right to vote.

> **The best thing about having a flat is being able to lock the door and feel safe. The second best thing is being able to vote. I got letters from the Labour, Conservative and Liberal Democrat parties just before the elections, because I could vote again now I had a home. I felt I had a say in my future again.**
>
> Dave, ex-homeless, aged 21

Being without an address can have other implications on a homeless person's rights. Article 23 of the Universal Declaration of Human Rights states 'Everyone has a right to work', but as we have seen (page 33), employment is very hard to find without an address. Many countries operate a system of registration and identity cards and, again, to register people often need an address and failing to register makes access to services, such as housing and benefits, hard to obtain. For example, in both Spain and Luxembourg, registration and proof of residency in a particular area (ie an address) are necessary to get the equivalent of income support.

The right to health care can also be denied through homelessness. In Britain, it is difficult to register with a doctor (general practitioner) because of being on the move and having no address. But it is not impossible. There are medical centres and day centres where homeless people can

Many of the day centres run by the churches offer medical care to the homeless on a regular weekly basis.

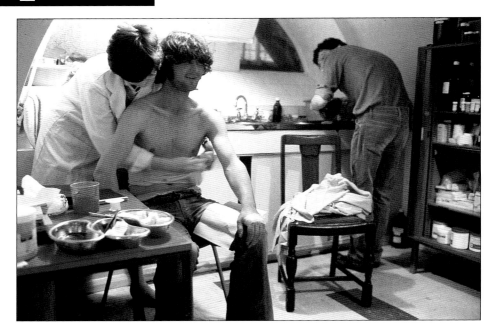

receive treatment from doctors, dentists, chiropodists and opticians. Long-term care can be hard to organise. GPs are encouraged to register homeless people, and more are doing so, but as one doctor explained:

'We will treat someone who is taken ill near the surgery who has been resident in the area less than 24 hours. This is called 'immediate necessary treatment'. But it is difficult to treat itinerant people because they are always moving on...there is no

> **66 Everyone has the right to social security. This includes shelter, health care and enough money on which to live. 99**
>
> Article 22, the Universal Declaration of Human Rights

continuous care or medical history to refer to. The nature of their lifestyle makes them more prone to long-term illness and there is no way we can follow up.'

THE RIGHT TO SHELTER?

Article 22 of the Universal Declaration of Human Rights is perhaps the most significant for the homeless (see panel, left). As we have seen, many homeless people fail to get access to the social security and benefits that the Article establishes as a right and, by definition, a homeless person is without a home and therefore without shelter. Some countries recognise the right to shelter by embodying it in their laws. Belgium and France are the only two countries in the European Union to do this, but even so, they have a long way to go to solve the problem.

FROM HUMAN RIGHTS TO LEGAL RIGHTS?

A woman and child without a home of their own sleep on the busy pavements of Paris.

Even if most countries recognise the Universal Declaration of Human Rights, it is up to the individual governments to uphold them in their legislation (law making). Translating the ideal into concrete law is a far harder task than simply establishing the ideals in the first place. A government must create laws that are practical to adminster, cost effective and, as far as possible, please the people who have elected them in the first place. Any law must also be as straightforward as possible, to avoid the possibility of differing interpretations, which in turn can lead to problems of access for the right people to the right services.

One piece of British legislation that has been criticised as hard to interpret is the Children Act of 1989. In accordance with a generally accepted human right, it states that local authorities are obliged to house and support homeless 16 and 17-year-olds in need. However, it is up to the local authority to decide what 'in need' means and opinions about this vary widely. A report issued by the Royal Philanthropic Society suggested that it was because of this that there were increasing social problems among the age group.

> **There exist many 'escape clauses' in legislation and practice whereby the public authorities' obligations are diluted or made ambiguous.**
>
> Third report of the European Observatory

> **" Unprecedented numbers of young people are being forced into crime, prostitution and drug dealing as a result of uncoordinated and flimsy government policies and the failure of the Children Act. "**
>
> *The Times*, in an article on the Royal Philanthropic Society's report

WHOSE RIGHT IS IT ANYWAY?

In order to protect the rights of one group of people, other groups may lose some things they consider to be their right. When the Criminal Justice Act was passed in Britain in 1994 its approach to people's rights provoked great controversy. The Act takes a tough line on crime and those who commit it, as well as introducing preventative measures to stop crime taking place. The Government argues that the Act gives the majority of people greater freedom and protects their rights. However, its critics have suggested that its severity has actually limited people's freedoms and given too much power to the police and people who own land or housing.

The Criminal Justice Act takes a severe stance on travellers, reflecting the negative attitude many people have towards them (see page 31). It makes it extremely difficult for anyone choosing to live an itinerant lifestyle. The police are empowered to act against people occupying land which does not belong to them, if the police think that their stay is not temporary.

The police have the power to remove trespassers forcibly if either the police or the landowner think that they have:

a) damaged the land or property;

b) used abusive or threatening behaviour to the landowner, or,

c) there is a group of more than six vehicles on the property.

The government says that these police powers are discretionary and will only be used if there are public order issues associated with illegal occupation, and they stress that the presence of elderly or pregnant women amongst the trespassers will be taken into account.

It would seem that if the human rights outlined here are to be respected, the travellers should be allowed to pursue their chosen lifestyle. But should they be allowed to do so at the expense of other people's right to own property and to protect it?

Squatters, too, are affected by the new act. In certain circumstances, it will become legal for any person to 'use or threaten violence for the purpose of securing entry' to premises that have been squatted. Any squatter refusing to leave in these circumstances can be arrested and imprisoned. Again, some people feel that this is a fair law, enabling people to

▶ page 52

> **" Everyone has the right to own property. No-one can take other people's possessions without a fair reason. "**
>
> Article 17, the Universal Declaration of Human Rights

Everyone has a right to travel and live anywhere in their home country. A person also has the right to leave any country, including his or her own, and to return to it.

Article 13, the Universal Declaration of Human Rights

Many New Age travellers feel that the Criminal Justice Act threatens their way of life.

protect their property, but others feel that by allowing violence to be used at all, the law is open to possible abuse. It might be hard to prove that excessive violence had been used, so the squatters themselves would be inadequately protected against this possibility.

The issues raised by considering people's rights are vast. In theory, the homeless should have the same rights as the rest of society but, in reality, these rights are often denied them. Sometimes the question of whose right it is can only be answered by the individual.

ARE THERE ANY SOLUTIONS?

There is no one solution to the problems of homelessness. At a general level, most people agree that the lack of affordable housing is a primary cause of homelessness but, as we saw in Chapter 2, there are many other contributory factors.

Providing the homeless with a roof is not the whole solution, although it must be seen as part of it. Many of the people are unable to cope alone when housed. They need continuing support to help them reintegrate into society and to regain their self-respect and confidence.

Long-term solutions, too, must not simply address the problem of those people who are homeless now but find ways to prevent people becoming homeless in the future.

HELPING THE HOMELESS DAY-TO-DAY

The homeless need help at two levels. Long-term solutions must be sought to the problem but immediate relief and assistance are also necessary. Much of this kind of day-to-day help is provided by non-governmental organisations (NGOs), which means that

Paula and Jean are ex-alcoholic and homeless women who have been housed in a rehabilitation flat. They can enjoy the comforts of a home for the first time in years.

although they may receive some financial help, they are not run by the government. Some NGOs are charities, some are linked to religious groups, others are voluntary.

In the UK, Shelter, Centrepoint, Crisis, St. Mungo Association and Char are a few amongst many of the organisations working for and with the homeless. They may help to provide a bed for the night, sponsor research programmes, training, produce educational material and organise events. Throughout the world organisations such as these exist, either on a national level, like the National Coalition for the Homeless in the USA, or on an international scale, like Oxfam.

The soup kitchens, day centres and hostels that these charities and groups provide are essential for day-to-day survival for many of the homeless. Not only do they provide food, shelter and health care, they also help the people who use them keep in touch with each other and continue to feel they are active members of our society.

Governments, too, have become involved with initiatives to provide immediate help for the homeless. This is partly a response to public pressure as homelessness has become increasingly visible in the developed world, with beggars on the streets, and people sleeping rough. It is especially

Day centres provide many facilities for the homeless, including the opportunity to learn a new skill such as screen printing.

apparent in colder climates over Christmas time, when public awareness is at a peak, but this does not always mean that there is on-going support during the rest of the year.

However, many governments do now recognise the problem as one that needs continuous attention. In London, the first phase of the Rough Sleepers Initiative (RSI) was launched in 1990 to help people sleeping rough. The British Government's aim was to make it unnecessary for anyone to have to sleep outdoors by the provision of additional hostels for accommodation and support via the voluntary sector.

Some other governments, too, have taken preventative measures. In Denmark, there is an early warning system. Social services must be notified before any family with children is evicted. Since April 1995 the Social Assistance Act obliges municipal authorities to provide shelter for single homeless people as well as families. A policy exists in Belgium where the local authorities can rehouse the homeless in property that has been vacant for more than six months.

Other government initiatives include an innovative scheme in the USA, where Federal Government programmes provide housing vouchers for homeless people (as well as those on very low income), which they give to their landlords to subsidise their rent. In New York City there is also a one-off special bonus paid to landlords who accept homeless people.

FINDING LONG-TERM SOLUTIONS

Some of these government initiatives are the start of what are hoped will be long-term solutions to homelessness. Here, too, the NGOs take an active part, particularly in the role of researchers and pressure groups. It is no coincidence that much of the information in this book has come from NGOs. They use the information they gather to put pressure on governments to amend their laws and policies to help the homeless. Most people recognise it is ultimately through government policies that long-term solutions to homelessness can be found: in the provision of social housing – with more affordable houses being built, finance and education.

It is the area of education that is a particular concern of those groups dealing with the problems of young homeless people. In the UK, Centrepoint constantly urges the need for young people to be educated at school in the realities of independent living. If young people understand their options when they leave home or care, appreciate the financial needs and know how to set about finding a job, they are less likely to run into some of the problems that can lead to homelessness. The personal and social education course (PSE) in schools is designed in part to help prepare students for leaving home.

Education can help to prevent young people becoming homeless, but many people feel that school leavers need far greater support than they currently receive, both financially and in access to training. How this can best be provided is the subject of a continuing debate between the many parties involved.

In 1989 FEANTSA (Fédération Européenne d'Associations Nationales Travaillant avec les Sans-Abri) was formed, funded by the European Commission. It is a pressure group whose long-term objectives are the reduction and elimination of homelessness in Europe. It seeks to do this through research and public information and by working closely with the institutions of the European Community.

> **Benefits to young people must be restored in full before the vicious cycle of destitution and homelessness blights more lives.**
>
> *We are human too, a study of people who beg*
> Alison Murdoch for Crisis

Since 1991, FEANTSA has been in charge of the European Observatory of Homelessness, which reported recently that the rights of the homeless in the countries of Europe were not as extensive as they could be.

FEANTSA saw the restoration of rights to the homeless through government legislation as one way towards a long-term solution to the problem. For example, they suggested that governments should recognise 'no fixed abode' as an official status enabling the homeless to overcome the many problems they encounter for lack of an address. They

> **There is evidence that the homeless can be deprived of that basic package of rights to which they are entitled and with respect to which they should be equal to other members of their society. Without such basic rights, people lack the entry ticket to participation in their society.**
>
> Third report of the European Observatory on Homelessness, 1994

also stressed the need for governments to continue to invest in social housing. As an international pressure group, they were able to point out examples of good and bad practice in the European Union.

WORKING TOGETHER

The relationship between governments and the NGOs can sometimes be tense and sometimes they will come into direct conflict with each other.

However, most people recognise that to achieve long-term solutions it is important for the NGOs, with all their knowledge and experience, to work together with the governments. One country that has done this successfully is Finland. Here the political authorities and the voluntary sector have joined together to help the homeless and in particular a special housing programme has been set up to provide 18,000 flats for homeless people.

In New York, deterioration of the commercial properties around Grand Central Station led to the local businesses becoming actively involved in dealing with the homeless situation. They formed an initiative called the Grand Central Partnership. The businesses paid a small tax and the funds were used to provide accommodation, training and job opportunities. The advantage for the businesses was to improve their environment and the advantage to the homeless was to improve their lives.

HELP YOURSELF

Some of the most successful initiatives for the homeless have one thing in common –

self-help. After the Second World War, Abbé Pierre, a priest (and former member of the Resistance) and later, a member of the French Parliament, started the Emmaus movement in France. It began when he first gave refuge to the homeless and encouraged them to recycle and sell things that others threw away. There are now over 350 Emmaus communities in 38 countries. Each member works to his or her ability for equal reward – food, clothing, shelter, and a modest cash allowance for personal needs.

In the United States, Habitat for Humanity gives homeless people an opportunity to help build a home of their own. The construction is carried out by volunteers who work alongside the homeless. It is an approach that is sometimes described as 'sweat equity': in return for their physical labour, people who would not otherwise own a home are given the opportunity to do so. At least 30,000 homes have been built in 42 countries since 1976.

Whilst some self-help schemes rely on labour, other self-help groups form political pressure groups. In India and Bangladesh, women's savings groups pool resources and lend money to each other at low interest rates. They also campaign together to protect their rights. Savita, whose story was told in Chapter 1 (see page 11), has become an active member of such a group.

SPREADING THE NEWS

Another self-help initiative that has been a success story is 'The Big Issue', a street paper sold by the homeless.

'The Big Issue' was launched in 1991 with the aim of helping the homeless to help themselves. Homeless vendors buy copies of the magazine for 30p and sell them to the public for 70p, keeping the profit. The magazine provides news, information on the arts, and the situation of the homeless today.

The Big Issue has provided over a thousand homeless people with a chance of earning a living for themselves since it started, five years ago.

> **" 1984 was an important year for us – we got our ration card, which enables us to get subsidised fuel and grain. I had joined a union of women pavement dwellers – Mahila Milan – to protest about our rights. Through this we managed to get this ration card. A few years later our homes were demolished and we lost all our possessions, everything. But with the help of the union, we took the State to court and were awarded compensation and we rebuilt our home here on the pavement. My family, and all the other families on the street, save some money each month through the union scheme in the hope of one day building a permanent home. What we really want is to have our own house. "**
>
> Savita

Besides highlighting major social issues and campaigning for the homeless, the 'Big Issue' offers training to vendors in writing, desk-top publishing and office skills. It helps refer people to specialist agencies for those who require help with drugs, alcohol or general conselling and it has a housing and resettlement unit offering advice, guidance, and accommodation.

'Street News' in New York was one of the first street papers to be produced. Now there are a number of other street papers operating in other parts of the world, creating opportunities for homeless people. In South Africa, 'Homeless Talk' is written by the homeless of Johannesburg. In France, 'La Rue' (The Street) is distributed throughout the country and in Hamburg, Germany, there is 'Hinz und Kunzt' (All and Sundry).

One of the reasons for the success of street papers for the homeless is that the general public find it much easier to buy a newspaper than just to give money to someone begging on the street. More importantly, it has raised the public awareness of the problems of the homeless, which in turn, gives fuel to the various pressure groups as they campaign for changes in the law and society as a whole.

It also provides a platform for the homeless to air their views within the pages. When the magazine began it had a circulation of 30,000 based around London with about 25 vendors. Five years later, the paper is being sold nationwide with a circulation of nearly a quarter of a million copies a week and the number of vendors has increased to well over 1000.

LEARNING FROM EACH OTHER

Some of the most original solutions to homelessness are to be found in the developing world. In several developing countries, Kenya and Brazil for example, people are allowed to squat or build on land that has been put aside for that

> **They need a hand up, not a hand out.**
>
> John Bird, Editor of *The Big Issue*

CAN WE HELP?

Having looked at a wide range of situations and causes of homelessness you will see that no one is insulated from this problem. The solutions are not easy, but the homeless can learn to help themselves and we can learn to help the homeless.

As young people you may be able to raise funds for organisations that help the homeless, buy street papers or support anyone you know who may be in danger of becoming one of Britain's homeless.

purpose. Over time, as and when resources become available, these buildings can slowly be made more permanent, adding utilities such as drainage and electricity. Slowly the areas become proper suburbs rather than squatter towns.

In Thailand, squatters are working with local businessmen and landowners in a sort of land-sharing. The squatters agree to keep off certain areas of land so they can be developed commercially, in return for help from the landowners with the installation of basic facilities in their homes. Some of these ideas are now being adopted by housing associations in Europe.

Find out
There are housing associations in nearly every area of Britain. Contact one local to you through your local authority and find out how they operate. Do they have any self-help schemes?

HELPLINE

HAMILTON COLLEGE

Telephone numbers beginning with 0800 are free and those beginning with 0345 are charged at local rate.

Childline
0800 1111
24-hour helpline for children and young people.

Citizen's Advice Bureaux
0171 833 2182
Free advice. More than 1000 local branches.

Children's Legal Centre
01206 873820

Message Home
0500 700 740
Free confidential helpline for people who want to contact their families.

NCH (National Children's Home) Action for Children
0171 226 2033
85 Highbury Park
London N5 1UD

Advice centres and help for those leaving care and the homeless.

NCH Wales
01222 222127
St David's Court
68A Crowbridge Road
East Cardiff CF1 9DN
(Advice centres, as above)

Continued on page 60

NCH Scotland
0141 332 4041
17 Newton Place
Glasgow G3 7PY
(Advice centres, as above)

National Children's Bureau
0171 843 6000
8 Wakely Street
London E1V 7QE
Provides information on where
to get help on a wide range of
issues.

National Youth Agency
0116 247 1200
17-23 Albion Street
Leicester LF1 6GD
Information shops for young
people around the country.

Samaritans
0171 285 6789
Local branches are listed in the
telephone directory.

Youth Access
0150 921 0420
Magazine Business Centre
11 Newarke Street
Leicester LF1 5SS
An association that will give
you the name and address of
an independent advice,
information and counselling
centre in your local area.

Centrepoint
0171 629 2229
2 Swallow Place
London W1
Provides 16-25 year-olds with
advice and immediate
accommodation.

London Connection
0171 930 3451
12 Adelaide Sreet
London WC2
Provides support for young
people aged 16-25 who are
homeless and unemployed.

PiCcadilly Advice Centre
0171 434 3773
Referral and advice for people
new to London or in need of
housing.

The Rainer Foundation
0181 694 9497
89 Blackheath Hill
London SE10 8TJ
Housing and support for young
mothers, homeless young
people and care leavers.

St. Mungo Association
0171 240 5431
83 Endell Street
London WC2
Accommodation and help for
homeless people.

IN CANADA

There are many hostels in each
city and town offering shelter to
the homeless. Organizations
offering assistance in local
communities:
— Community Services
  Department
— YMCA
— YWCA
— Society of Saint Vincent de
  Paul
— The Salvation Army
— Jewish Family Services
— Children's Aid Society
— Catholic Children's Aid
  Society

IN AUSTRALIA

The Smith Family
National headquarters
16 Larkin Street
Camperdown, NSW 2050
Ph (008) 024 069 or (02) 550
4422

The Salvation Army

VICTORIA Box 1287k GPO
          Melbourne, VIC 3001
          Ph (03) 9698 7222

N.S.W.   P.O. Box A229
         Sydney South,
         NSW 2000
         Ph (02) 266 9631

QLD   GPO Box 1111
         Brisbane, QLD 4001
         Ph (07) 3222 6666

S.A.   Box 128 Rundle Mall
         P.O.
         Adelaide, S.A. 5000
         Ph (08) 223 1324

TAS   Box 487E P.O.
         Hobart, Tas 7001
         Ph (002) 344 333

W.A.   Box 8498 P.O.
         Stirling Street
         Perth, W.A. 6849
         Ph (09) 227 7010

A.C.T   P.O. Box 4224
         Kingston ACT 2604
         Ph (06) 27 33055

INDEX